Norman Winegar, LCSW
L. Michelle Hayter, MSW

Guidebook to Managed Care and Practice Management Terminology

Pre-publication REVIEWS, COMMENTARIES, EVALUATIONS . . .

"**W**inegar and Hayter's *Guidebook to Managed Care and Practice Management Terminology* is an essential companion to Winegar's previous text, *The Clinician's Guide to Managed Behavioral Care* (Haworth, 1996). Defining clinical, financial, management, and utilization review terms in crisp and simple language, this book will need to be in the desk drawer of every healthcare manager and practitioner in this brave new world of managed care."

Paul A. Kurzman, PhD
Professor, Hunter College School of Social Work, City University of New York

"**T**he School of Social Work is proud to be associated with this book, which is the product of a creative convergence of student learning objectives, field instructor expertise, and agency support. Every profession has its jargon . . . initials and acronyms are bandied about freely as we use our professional short-hand to communicate. This guidebook is just that, a thorough, but concise, definitional map that will be helpful for students and novice practitioners as they negotiate and communicate in the managed care practice environment."

Jaclyn Miller, PhD, LCSW
Director of Field Instruction, Virginia Commonwealth University, School of Social Work, Richmond, VA

The Haworth Press
New York • London

Guidebook to Managed Care and Practice Management Terminology

HAWORTH Marketing Resources
Innovations in Practice & Professional Services
William J. Winston, Senior Editor

New, Recent, and Forthcoming Titles:

Strategic Planning for Not-for-Profit Organizations by R. Henry Migliore, Robert E. Stevens, and David L. Loudon

Marketing Planning in a Total Quality Environment by Robert E. Linneman and John L. Stanton, Jr.

Managing Sales Professionals: The Reality of Profitability by Joseph P. Vaccaro

Squeezing a New Service into a Crowded Market by Dennis J. Cahill

Publicity for Mental Health Clinicians: Using TV, Radio, and Print Media to Enhance Your Public Image by Douglas H. Ruben

Managing a Public Relations Firm for Growth and Profit by A. C. Croft

Utilizing the Strategic Marketing Organization: The Modernization of the Marketing Mindset by Joseph P. Stanco

Internal Marketing: Your Company's Next Stage of Growth by Dennis J. Cahill

The Clinician's Guide to Managed Behavioral Care by Norman Winegar

Marketing Health Care into the Twenty-First Century: The Changing Dynamic by Alan K. Vitberg

Fundamentals of Strategic Planning for Health-Care Organizations edited by Stan Williamson, Robert Stevens, David Loudon, and R. Henry Migliore

Risky Business: Managing Violence in the Workplace by Lynne Falkin McClure

Predicting Successful Hospital Mergers and Acquisitions: A Financial and Marketing Analytical Tool by David P. Angrisani and Robert L. Goldman

Marketing Research That Pays Off: Case Histories of Marketing Research Leading to Success in the Marketplace edited by Larry Percy

How Consumers Pick a Hotel: Strategic Segmentation and Target Marketing by Dennis Cahill

Applying Telecommunications and Technology from a Global Business Perspective by Jay Zajas and Olive Church

Strategic Planning for Private Higher Education by Carle M. Hunt, Kenneth W. Oosting, Robert Stevens, David Loudon, and R. Henry Migliore

Writing for Money in Mental Health by Douglas H. Ruben

The New Business Values for Success in the Twenty-First Century: Improvement, Innovation, Inclusion, Incentives, Information by John Persico and Patricia Rouner Morris

Marketing Planning Guide, Second Edition by Robert E. Stevens, David L. Loudon, Bruce Wrenn, and William E. Warren

Contemporary Sales Force Management by Tony Carter

4 × 4 Leadership and the Purpose of the Firm by H. H. Pete Bradshaw

Lessons in Leisure Business Success: The Recreation Professional's Business Transformation Primer by Jonathan T. Scott

Guidebook to Managed Care and Practice Management Terminology by Norman Winegar and Michelle L. Hayter

Medical Group Management in Turbulent Times: How Physician Leadership Can Optimize Health Plan, Hospital, and Medical Group Performance by Paul A. Sommers

Defining Your Market: Winning Strategies for High-Tech, Industrial, and Service Firms by Art Weinstein

Defective Bosses: Working for the Dysfunctional Dozen by Kerry Carson and Paula Phillips Carson

Guidebook to Managed Care and Practice Management Terminology

Norman Winegar, LCSW
L. Michelle Hayter, MSW

The Haworth Press
New York • London

The Haworth Press, Inc., 10 Alice Street, Binghamton, NY 13904-1580

Cover design by Marylouise E. Doyle.

Library of Congress Cataloging-in-Publication Data

Winegar, Norman.
    Guidebook to managed care and practice management terminology / Norman Winegar, L. Michelle Hayter.
        p.   cm.
    Includes bibliographical references and index.
    ISBN 0-7890-0447-X (alk. paper).
    1. Managed care plans (Medical care)—Terminology. I. Hayter, L. Michelle. II. Title.
RA413.W48 1998
362.1′04258′014—dc21   98-12222
                                                                                                          CIP

CONTENTS

ABOUT THE AUTHORS

Norman Winegar, LCSW, CEAP, is Regional Director for Professional Practice for MCC Behavioral Care, Inc., in Richmond, Virginia. He has been a clinical administrator in the managed care field for over ten years. A frequent presenter and trainer, Mr. Winegar has published numerous papers on topics concerning chemical dependency treatment, employee assistance programming, and managed care. He is co-author of *Marketing Mental Health Services to Managed Care.*

L. Michelle Hayter, MSW, is a recent graduate of the Virginia Commonwealth University School of Social Work in Richmond, Virginia. As a student, she completed a planning and administrative internship at MCC Behavioral Care, Inc. She is currently employed by Paralyzed Veterans of America.

Preface

During the 1996-1997 academic year, Michelle Hayter, along with Tanya Noble, were graduate Social Work Administration students at MCC Behavioral Care in Richmond, Virginia. Mr. Winegar was their Field Instructor. That placement afforded the students an opportunity for learning about the overall operations of managed care organizations, particularly in the areas of practice management, financial processes, quality management structures and activities, and clinical service delivery, including employee assistance programs.

The genesis of this book arose from the need for a concise and practical glossary of managed care terminology. It is intended to supplement the wide range of readings about this emerging and important field that is of so much interest to graduate and undergraduate students in the human service and healthcare fields.

Acknowledgments

The authors wish to thank and acknowledge the following individuals and organizations for their support of this book: Virginia Commonwealth University's School of Social Work and its Field Instruction department, for offering managed care organizations as placement opportunities for social work graduate students; MCC Behavioral Care, for providing graduate social work administration students with placements at its Richmond, Virginia offices; Dr. Jacki Miller and Dr. Ellen Netting of the VCU School of Social Work for their support, guidance, and advice in the development of this project and for their commitment to the provision of rewarding and innovative instructional options for graduate students; Susan Sheridan, MS, LPC, CEAP, a clinical administrator at MCC Behavioral Care who was instrumental in supporting and supervising the students in the area of clinical quality management activities; John Bistline, EdD, LCP, CEAP, the Practice Director and all the staff of MCC's Richmond offices; and finally, thanks to Roderick Hafer, PhD, a senior executive at MCC Behavioral Care, whose leadership has for many years created an atmosphere that encourages quality and innovation in fulfilling the important mission of delivering behavioral care services to consumers and employers.

Introduction

A revolution has transformed the healthcare delivery system in the United States. It has forever altered the landscape of clinical practice in a wide variety of professional disciplines. Always controversial, frequently successful, sometimes spectacularly disappointing, and never quiet, this revolution has also impacted consumers, purchasers, practitioners, and students. It is the revolution of managed care, and it has fundamentally changed the way in which America's healthcare services are financed, managed, marketed, and delivered.

This revolution has not been without upheaval. Beginning as a trickle of change during the 1970s, federal legislation stimulated the growth of health maintenance organizations, which had formerly been largely a regional anomaly in a tradition-bound system of healthcare. These structures introduced notions of discounted fees, primary care physicians as gatekeepers and case managers, restrictions in the choice of providers and facilities, and reduced claims paperwork for consumers.

The trickle soon became a torrent of change during the 1980s. During that decade, HMOs and their kindred proliferated both in form and in geographical dispersion. Purchasers eagerly pursued them as a means to combat the seemingly out-of-control medical inflation—inflation perceived as a threat to American business' competitiveness, both domestically and globally. Such financial and care delivery systems expanded into areas of dental care and behavioral care at a time when consumers came to expect wider coverage for conditions previously not covered by employer-sponsored benefit plans, or conditions that were once ignored or stigmatized.

Employee assistance programs multiplied, sometimes in response to the perception of diminished access to services due to managed care systems, sometimes as a means of supplementing managed care systems with an employer-sponsored prevention and early intervention tool. New professional groups began to be reimbursed in these systems, and new treatments emphasizing cost-effectiveness and outpatient treatment modalities were promoted. By late in the decade, the private psychiatric hospital boom had become a contraction as managed care shortened stays and diverted patients to alternative care settings. But the revolution was just starting.

During the 1990s, the revolution has continued gaining wide acceptance for many of its structures and processes. It has been embraced by public sector treatment systems, themselves faced with the crisis of seemingly endless need for services and diminishing resources to provide for them. Managed care's acceptance by the purchaser community, be it public or private, has been due in large part to its ability to control costs of clinical services.

However, the prevalence and growth of managed care systems has not come without a price. A consumer and professional backlash to these changes has resulted in increased awareness, political action, regulation, oversight, litigation, and controversy. Managed care systems have also resulted in a change of expectations on the part of purchasers. No longer content with containing costs and controlling medical inflation, purchasers today expect much more from the revolution. They expect lower costs *and* better customer service, better treatment outcomes, enhanced quality and oversight, better alignment with purchaser objectives on the part of treatment professionals, and a recognition by managed care systems that many stakeholders have interests in their success or shortcomings.

One key stakeholder in this revolution is the large community of treatment professionals who organize, manage, evaluate, and deliver clinical services to Americans. To them, the managed care revolution has represented the industrialization of healthcare—a marked change from the largely cottage industry of service delivery of a generation ago.

During that time, healthcare was mostly the domain of individual practitioners and governmental and nonprofit entities. Patients were seldom viewed as active consumers with their own stake in the system. Accountability and oversight of practice was limited. Professional autonomy and patient choice of practitioner were maximal. Treatment plans for similar presentations varied according to the clinician's training and knowledge. Reimbursement systems were focused on indemnity insurance mechanisms or governmental support. A fragmented system of isolated practitioners prevailed. The paradigm of healthcare as a competitive business, with active, educated consumers, integrated delivery systems, product innovation, practice standardization, a focus on outcomes, and efficiency of processes was absent. Managed care has represented the introduction of these principles to an area of American life from which they were historically devoid. For a generation of skilled practitioners and professionals, this has been a challenging transition.

As with other revolutions, a new vocabulary of often bewildering terms, acronyms, and concepts has been created. Sometimes to the consternation of both veteran practitioners and students alike, fluency in this vocabulary is the currency of clinical practice today.

Regardless of professional discipline, practice setting, or clinical training, familiarity with this terminology is essential in the merging world of healthcare practice and business. However, these terms are too often absent from training texts and are difficult to compile from even an extensive perusal of the literature of journals, newsletters, and professional magazines. The ambitious goal of this book is to provide readers with a handy and concise compilation of the most commonly used terms and acronyms needed to do business with managed care systems and to navigate successfully in the healthcare practice world today.

In pursuing this goal, only the terms and acronyms most commonly used and most relevant to practice in managed care environments were selected for inclusion. The intended audience for this book includes students and practitioners in the field of social work and the other health and human service professions who are interested in learning about practice in managed care settings or in doing business in a marketplace dominated by managed care. Consumers interested in navigating healthcare systems' technical terminology will also find this work helpful.

For ease of use, the terms and concepts have been arranged into broad headings that concern four key areas for today's successful clinical practitioner: clinical terminology, financial terminology, practice management terminology, and quality management and utilization review terms. Terms are arranged alphabetically. Italicized words within definitions represent cross-references. Also included is a section of resources, both government and private agencies, that can provide further information on healthcare and healthcare policy. In an effort to remain as current as possible, Internet addresses have been included wherever applicable.

We hope this book proves to be a useful supplement in the study of America's complex and evolving healthcare system.

Clinical Terms and Concepts

activities of daily living (ADL): Functions that must be performed or supported, at a minimum, to sustain an individual. These functions include bathing, dressing, toileting, transferring, continence, and feeding. Treatment plans and treatment updates to MCOs identify the impact of diagnostic conditions on patients' ADL and how professional services are assisting the patient in returning to premorbid ADL levels.

assessed problem: Refers to the physician or the clinician's diagnosis of the patient's problem. Determined by the clinician, the assessed problem may differ from the patient's *presenting problem.*

attending physician: The physician with the primary responsibility for the care provided to a patient in a hospital or other healthcare facility. In MCO systems, the attending physician is viewed as the preferred primary contact for the MCO case manager, while the patient is in the acute level of care setting.

board certification: An indicator that a physician has passed an examination given by a medical specialty board and has met other eligibility requirements that certify the physician as a specialist in a particular area. Thus, the physician is "board certified." Board certification is often a requirement for credentialing by many MCOs.

Many veteran psychiatrists are not board certified due to the status of certification systems in years past. Today, however, most MCOs routinely require psychiatrists to be board certified for credentialing in MCO behavioral care networks.

Board certification is available in the other mental health fields as well, although its value to MCOs is not as clearly perceived, as is the case of psychiatry. Many of these professions have only recently gained the level of acceptance needed for state licensure for autonomous practice, a minimal credentialing of MCOs. Some professions such as social work have competing certification bodies which cloud the value of certification further to purchasers and consumers—who ultimately influence network credentialing criteria.

C
care management/case management: A coordinated set of professional activities focused on treatment planning and the assurance of treatment delivery that addresses patients' biopsychosocial needs and achieves quality, cost-effective outcomes. Also termed *case management.*

In the MCO environment, care managers review treatment plans, perform precertification duties, authorize benefit coverage for services, and consult with professionals providing direct care to clients. Care management is an increasingly automated process with care managers having access to provider profile information, databases of network services available to clients, records pertaining to past treatment episodes, and clinical decision support tools. Most care management is conducted by registered nurses in medical MCOs and in behavioral MCOs by social workers supported by psychiatrists.

catastrophic case management: Occurs when a patient is having a difficult or severe problem that may require extended or costly periods of care, or is close to exhausting the patient's insurance benefits.

chronic illness: Refers to diseases or conditions, usually of slow progress and long continuance, requiring ongoing care. In behavioral health, chronic illness is often referred to as serious and persistent mental illness (SPMI).

clinical care: The provision of healthcare services, both medical and behavioral healthcare, including utilization management and case management services. This type of care can be contrasted to *member/customer/consumer services*. Measures of clinical care include *continuity of care*, which refers to the provision of care by the same set of clinicians to a member over time. If the same clinicians are not available over time, a mechanism is necessary to provide appropriate clinical information in a timely fashion to the clinicians who continue to provide the same type and level of care. Another measure is *coordination of clinical care*, which refers to the mechanisms assuring that the member and clinicians take into consideration and have access to all the required information on the member's conditions and treatments, ensuring that the member receives appropriate healthcare services.

clinical peer: A physician or other healthcare professional who holds a nonrestricted license in a state in the United States and in the same or similar specialty as typically manages the medical condition, procedures, or treatment under review. Generally as a peer in a similar specialty, the individual should be in the same profession and the same licensure category as the practitioner on whom the review is being done.

clinical privileges: Authorization by an appropriate authority for a practitioner to provide defined patient care services in the organization, based on the practitioner's license, education, training, experience, competence, ability to perform requested privileges, and judgment.

clinical rationale: A statement that provides additional clarification of the clinical basis for a *noncertification* determination to the patient's condition or treatment plan. A clinical rationale should supply a sufficient basis for a decision to pursue an appeal.

clinical review criteria: The written screens, decision trees, or other protocols used by a utilization review organization to determine *medical necessity* and *level of care* decisions. Some MCOs such as MCC Behavioral Care—the behavioral care unit of Philadelphia-based insurance company CIGNA—offer their review criteria to their affiliated network providers and conduct training activities around them.

clinicians: Medical healthcare and behavioral healthcare providers.

comorbidity: This term refers to coexisting (and usually chronic) conditions that may affect the overall health and functional status of an individual, beyond the effect or effects of the condition under consideration. For example, in behavioral health, the simultaneous appearance of two or more illnesses such as alcohol dependence and depression indicates comorbidity.

covered services: Professional services of physicians, hospitals, and other providers that have been authorized by the healthplan or MCO. Covered services may vary by benefit plan, causing confusion on the part of clients and professionals, including those charged with administering them. MCOs commonly administer numerous and varying benefit plans. For example, Plan A covers V Code diagnoses, but Plan B does not. Formerly a member of Plan A, Mr. Smith attended marital therapy, which was covered by his employer-sponsored mental health benefit plan two years ago. Last year Mr. Smith's employer switched to Plan B, an HMO whose behavioral care benefits exclude marital therapy for Mr. Smith's V Code diagnosis, for which he now presents. The Smiths and their clinical social worker therapist are surprised and confused when they learn that marital therapy is now not a covered service.

custodial care: Care designed to assist an individual to meet his/her activities of daily living. These activities do not entail or require the continuing attention of trained medical or paramedical personnel.

D **date of service:** Date on which the health services (or other covered services) are provided.

Department of Transportation regulations: The name commonly applied to a complex set of regulations governing the workforces of industries that employ workers in safety sensitive roles such as the airline, trucking, and public transportation industries. These regulations require that workers who test positive for illicit drug use are referred to a substance abuse professional for screening for substance abuse education or treatment services.

***Diagnostic and Statistical Manual—Fourth Edition* (DSM-IV):** The American Psychiatric Association's manual of diagnostic criteria and terminology, widely accepted as the common language of behavioral health clinicians and researchers.

disability: The inability to perform all or some portion of the duties of one's occupation or, alternatively, any occupation as a result of a physical or mental impairment. Long-term disability (LTD) occurs when the period of disability becomes significant, generally ranging from six months to life. Short-term disability (STD) occurs when the period of disability is temporary, usually less than six months. Partial disability is a disability that prevents an employee from performing one or more, but not necessarily all, material duties of his or her job.

discharge planning: The process that assesses a patient's needs in order to help arrange for the necessary services and resources to effect an appropriate and timely discharge. In today's treatment environment, heavily influenced by MCO systems with shorter lengths of stay, the collaborative process of discharge planning must commence almost as soon as the admission is complete. The MCO case manager with knowledge of all the network's resources can be a valuable adjunct to the hospital-based treatment team as they jointly pursue a treatment plan that facilitates a discharge to the level of care required by each patient.

dual diagnosis: In behavioral health, the co-occurrence within one's lifetime of a psychiatric disorder and a substance use disorder. The preferred medical term is *comorbidity*.

durable medical equipment: Equipment that can withstand repeated use and is usually not useful to a person in the absence of illness or injury. It is also appropriate for use in the home. To be covered, durable medical equipment must be *medically necessary* and prescribed by a participating physician for use in the home.

*E***lective:** Healthcare or other services that can be delayed without substantial risk to the health of the patient. Elective services are typically not considered *medically necessary* by MCOs and are therefore not covered by benefits.

emergency services: Inpatient or outpatient services that are needed immediately because of sudden injury or illness.

emergent/emergency admission: Admission that occurs directly from the hospital emergency room.

encounter: An episode of service, a member's encounter with a healthcare provider. Health maintenance organizations keep encounter data—particularly when there are no claims generated because the provider has received a capitation payment from that member.

end stage renal disease (ESRD): Diagnosis that automatically makes a person eligible for Medicare insurance coverage regardless of age. Beneficiaries usually require kidney dialysis or a kidney transplant to sustain life.

experimental procedures and items: Items and procedures determined not to be generally accepted practice in the medical community.

extended care facility: A medical care institution for members who require long-term custodial or medical care, especially for chronic disease or a condition requiring prolonged rehabilitation therapy.

F **facility provider:** a hospital, pharmacy, clinic, partial hospital, or intensive outpatient treatment program that contracts with a managed care organization. Contrasts with a professional *provider* or group of professionals.

I **inpatient care:** Care given a registered bed patient in a hospital or an extended care facility, nursing home, or other medical or psychiatric institution.

intensive outpatient program (IOP): In behavioral healthcare, an IOP refers to an outpatient treatment program that provides two to four hours of care, two or more times a week, including both individual and group therapy.

intervention: An action taken by an organization or a practitioner to increase the probability that desired *outcomes* will occur.

L **level of care:** The term for treatment alternatives on a continuum of care that includes inpatient, partial or day hospitalization, outpatient, and long-term residential treatment or group home situations.

long-term care facility: Facility designed to provide long-term or custodial care to persons unable to be cared for in the home environment, but not requiring the intensive or skilled care of a hospital.

long-term disability (LTD): A significant period of disability, usually defined as more than six months, in which an employee cannot work but is eligible for partial benefits and salary.

M **mental health services:** A wide range of diagnostic, therapeutic, and rehabilitative services used in the treatment of mental health and/or substance abuse.

mental illness: Any disorder that impairs the behavior, emotional reaction, or thought process of a person, regardless of medical origin.

multidisciplinary: Utilizing professional practitioners with a wide range of specialties.

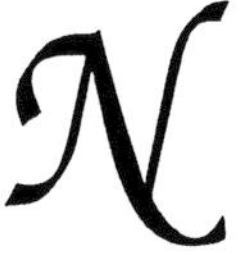 **neonatal care:** The care provided to a newborn within the first six weeks of life, or prolonged care for an infant who has abnormal health problems.

occupational medicine department: An entity common to large employers which provides a variety of health services and is often the point of interface between the employer, EAP, and disability management vendors.

occupational therapy: Therapeutic use of work, self-care, and play activities to increase independent functions, enhance development, prevent disability, and achieve maximum independence.

office visit: Formal face-to-face contact between the provider and the patient in a healthcare environment.

outcome: The behavioral results achieved through the performance of a treatment process, intervention, or course of therapy.

outpatient care: All health services provided to a member who is not admitted to any inpatient facility. Outpatient care can be provided in a physician or therapist's office, a clinic, a member's home, or a hospital outpatient department.

oversight: The monitoring and direction of a set of activities, resulting in the achievement of desired outcomes.

overutilization: Provision of services that were not clearly indicated, or provision of services that were indicated in either excessive amounts or in a higher level setting than required.

P **partial hospitalization:** A structural or "day treatment" alternative providing four to twelve hours of care per day. This *level of care* is frequently seen as a "follow-up" or transitional treatment after inpatient care.

patient-specific information: Information that is sufficient to allow for identification of the individual patient. This information is not routinely available to employers or purchasers of medical or behavioral care benefits without the permission of the client.

physical therapy: Rehabilitation concerned with restoration of function and prevention of physical disability following disease or a debilitating injury.

physician attestation: A prescribed, federally mandated statement assuring that the description of the principal and secondary diagnoses and procedures in a medical record are accurate. This statement must be signed and dated by the attending physician and be present in the medical record.

practice guidelines: Recommended therapies and procedures for the treatments of specific disorders so as to achieve optimum results as efficiently as possible. They are not rigid standards; rather, they are suggestions that offer supportive guidance to clinicians. Practice guidelines are developed from the clinical literature, professional societies, and/or through other clinician input forums. Practice guidelines are designed to help providers and patients make decisions, and many managed care organizations use such guidelines for *quality assurance* or *accountability* purposes to determine *appropriateness and medical necessity* of care.

preexisting condition: A condition that existed, or for which a participant was being treated, before coverage under a current health or disability plan commenced, and for which benefits under the plan may be unavailable or limited.

presenting problem: Patients' own diagnoses or descriptions in their own words of their problem. The presenting problem may be different from the *assessed problem.*

prevalence: A rate expressing the number of existing (both new and old) occurrences of a particular condition within an at-risk population at a specific point or during a specific period of time.

preventive care: Care designed for disease prevention. The aim of preventive care is to detect and treat disease at an early stage or to manage its course most effectively. Examples of preventive care include immunizations and regular screenings such as Pap smears or cholesterol checks. Controversy exists in the healthcare fields as to the cost benefits of various prevention-oriented activities and initiatives.

primary care: Preventive healthcare and routine medical care provided on an outpatient basis that is typically provided by a doctor trained in internal medicine, pediatrics, or family practice, or by a nurse, nurse practitioner, or physician's assistant.

primary prevention: Activities undertaken to prevent the occurrence of a mental disorder by eliminating causative agents, removing risk factors, and enhancing patient competence. For example, the provision of parenting classes, alcohol and drug education, and stress management programs.

principal diagnosis: The condition that, after study, is determined to be the primary reason for admission to the healthcare delivery system.

principal procedure: A procedure performed for definitive treatment rather than one performed for diagnostic or exploratory purposes, or that is necessary to treat a complication. The principal procedure is the procedure most related to the principal diagnosis.

R **referral:** A formal process that authorizes an HMO member to get care from a *specialist* or a *hospital.* To ensure coverage, an HMO member generally must get a referral from his or her *primary care physician* before seeing a *specialist.* A referral can also involve the sending of an individual from one setting or service to another.

referral physician: Any doctor to whom a member is specifically referred for health services by the healthcare plan or a primary care physician (PCP) after obtaining prior authorization.

rehabilitation: A broad range of physical, mental, and social activities (long-term or short-term) designed to restore an individual to the highest possible functional capacity after an episode of illness or injury; examples of rehabilitation include physical therapy, speech therapy, occupational therapy, chiropractic therapy, and family counseling.

rehabilitative therapy: Physical, speech, and occupational therapy provided on an inpatient or outpatient basis. Such rehabilitation is available only if *medically necessary,* prescribed by a doctor, periodically reviewed by a doctor, and part of a plan of treatment set up by a doctor or therapist.

S **screening:** Process in which norms, criteria, and standards are used to analyze cases in order to identify those requiring further study.

second surgical opinion: Concurring opinion from a second surgeon required by some insurance plans prior to authorizing a surgical procedure.

secondary prevention: Activities undertaken to ensure early identification and prompt treatment of an illness or disorder, with the goal of reducing the prevalence of the condition and shortening its duration. For example, early identification and treatment of attention deficit-hyperactivity disorder.

sentinel diagnosis: A marker condition where timely and appropriate medical management, member education, and other outpatient therapies should result in members being managed successfully in the ambulatory setting with little need for hospitalizations.

short-term disability (STD): A temporary period, generally less than six months, in which an employee is unable to work but is eligible for partial benefits and salary. Employers are increasingly aware of the costs of STD, particularly the impact of STD cases related to behavioral disorders and conditions. MCOs and EAPs offer disability management products to facilitate effective management of STD benefits.

skilled nursing facility: An institution whose services are furnished by, or are under general supervision of, licensed nursing personnel under the general direction of a physician, whose responsibility is to assure the safety of members and achieve stated medically desired results.

specialist: A physician whose training and expertise are in a specific area of medicine, such as oncology or radiology, that provides certain specialty medical care. Usually, most HMO members require a referral by the primary care physician (PCP) and authorization from the HMO in order to see a specialist.

speech therapy: The study, diagnosis, and treatment of defects and disorders of the voice and of spoken and written communication.

substance abuse professional (SAP): A term used in the context of Department of Transportation regulations governing industries employing workers in safety sensitive positions. These regulations require such employees who are tested positive for a variety of illicit drugs to be assessed for possible substance abuse treatment services by an SAP. Such professionals may be EAP professionals, certified substance abuse counselors, physicians, psychologists, or licensed clinical social workers. MCOs and EAP companies organize and credential such specialty networks and market them to employers.

T **tertiary prevention:** Activities undertaken to reduce impairment or disability following the development of a disorder. For psychiatric conditions, tertiary prevention involves efforts to enable those with serious and persistent mental illnesses to reach their highest level of functioning.

treatment episode: The period of treatment between admission and discharge from a modality; e.g., inpatient, residential, partial hospitalization, and outpatient. Healthcare statistics and profiles commonly use this unit as a base for comparisons. Many disorders in both the medical and the behavioral care fields require multiple treatment episodes over the course of a patient's lifetime.

treatment plan: A written action plan, based on assessment data, that identifies the patient's clinical needs, the strategy for providing services to meet those needs, treatment goals and objectives, and the criteria for terminating the specified interventions.

treatment record: The record in which clinical information related to the provision of physical, social, and mental health services is recorded and stored.

triage: Taking appropriate action to address a crisis situation or a clinical emergency. In behavioral health, referral and triage staff determine the degree of clinical urgency and the appropriate setting of care.

Financial Terms and Concepts

A **actuary:** A professional who determines insurance policy rates, reserves, and dividends, and also conducts various other statistical studies. This professional mathematically analyzes and prices the risks associated with providing insurance coverage and calculates the costs of providing future benefits. The statistical analysis involves the morbidity and mortality rates associated with the group to be insured, along with the underlying costs, administrative expenses, and anticipated investment returns.

administrative services only (ASO) fee: A common type of fee arrangement in the managed care industry, marked by an MCO being paid a fixed fee per covered life, per month, for the provision of administrative rather than clinical services. These administrative services may include preadmission certification, care management, utilization reviews, eligibility determination, claims administration, and data reporting. This type of financial arrangement may be used when the purchaser, usually an employer or labor organization, wishes to maintain the responsibility for the financial risk of actual services provided. The successful administration of an ASO contract presupposes an existing, efficient administrative infrastructure. The vendor organization may gain fee-for-service revenues from the provision of clinical services in instances in which the MCO provides services via a staff model. More often the MCO's administrative fee includes its cost of providing network access, precertification and concurrent review services, and/or a claim payment, while the actual cost of clinical services is charged to the purchaser. Performance assurances, which may put some or all of the fee at risk if not met, are often a part of such arrangements between MCOs and their customers. See *administrative services only fee, with risk sharing.*

administrative services only (ASO) fee, with risk sharing: In addition to the characteristics of the *ASO fee*, this arrangement between the purchaser and vendor organization stipulates one or more service targets, which, if not met, result in a penalty (usually in the form of a monetary rebate to the purchaser). Targets may involve inpatient or outpatient utilization, claims payment turnaround time, or accuracy or customer service targets, such as telephone answering responsiveness.

admissions per 1,000: An indicator calculated by taking the total number of inpatient and/or outpatient admissions from a specific group (such as an employer group or HMO population) for a specific period of time (usually one year), dividing it by the average number of covered members in that group during the same period, and multiplying the result by 1,000. This indicator can be calculated for behavioral health or any disease in the aggregate, as well as by modality of treatment (inpatient, residential, partial hospitalization, etc.). Such measures are commonly used by managed care entities to evaluate utilization management performance: the number of admissions (per year) / number of covered individuals (per year) $\times$ 1000 equals the admissions per 1,000 members.

at risk: The financial liability that an entity has to pay for all treatment for a given population in return for a fixed monthly fee.

at-risk capitation: In this increasingly commonplace financial arrangement, the purchaser of managed care services pays the provider organization or group a fixed fee per covered member per month (PMPM). In return, the managed care organization or provider group is "at risk" for the administrative and clinical service delivery costs associated with the provision of care to an identified consumer population group eligible for specified healthcare benefits. The monthly payment fluctuates only as the size of the population changes, allowing the purchaser (i.e., an HMO or employer) to predict and budget its healthcare costs, while providing incentives to the managed care organization to provide cost-effective care along a continuum of service offerings.

audit of provider treatment or charges: A qualitative or quantitative review of services rendered or proposed by a healthcare provider. The review may be carried out in a number of ways: a comparison of patient records and claim form information, a patient questionnaire, a review of hospital and practitioner records, or a pre- or posttreatment clinical examination of a patient. Such audits are increasingly used as part of MCOs' quality management programs.

B **balance billing:** The practice of charging full fees in excess of covered amounts, then billing the patient for that portion of the bill that the payer does not cover.

C **capitation:** The amount of money paid to an insurer, a physician, medical group, or ancillary provider to provide a specific set of services on a per member per month (PMPM) basis. This system, devised as a cost-containment function, contrasts with traditional indemnity insurance which generally reimburses on a per-procedure basis. Capitation arrangements, though commonplace today, remain controversial, as some believe they promote the withholding of needed services.

carve-outs: A benefit strategy in which an employer separates ("carves out") the mental health and substance abuse portion of healthcare benefits from others and contracts with a managed behavioral care (MBC) company to manage or provide the benefits through its networks. This type of strategy affords the employer with specialized management for this portion of the overall benefits package. Carve-outs became common for large employers during the late 1980s as a means of offering a customized behavioral care benefit program in addition to or in concert with an HMO offering for their workforces.

case rate: A flat fee paid to a practitioner or facility for clients' treatment based on their diagnoses and/or presenting problems. For this fee, the provider or facility provides all of the services the clients require for a specific period of time. This is a type of financial risk-sharing arrangement. In this arrangement, a family therapist might negotiate a case rate of $500 per referral from an MCO and would provide all necessary treatment services for the individual, couple, or family member. Such arrangements are favored for their administrative simplicity. The MCO monitors the quality of services delivered to ensure satisfactory outcomes and client satisfaction.

churning: A form of *code gaming* where the same procedure is billed more than once.

claimant: An enrollee or covered person who files a claim for benefits.

claims administrator: Any entity that reviews and pays claims to enrollees or providers of care on behalf of health benefit plans. These may be insurance companies, managed mental healthcare corporations, third-party administrators, self-insured employers, or other contractors.

code gaming: The use of incorrect billing codes to increase provider income or to enable a member to receive reimbursement for a treatment that would otherwise be nonreimbursable.

coinsurance/copayment: A provision in some health insurance policies, including Medicare, that specifies that the policyholder will share payment of covered services, either as a fixed sum (copayment) or a percentage (coinsurance). Some MCOs have policies and protocols for the disenrollment (expulsion) of providers who waive such payments or of members who do not make such payments.

collections per 1,000: An indicator calculated by taking the total collections for services received by a specific group (e.g., employer group or group for which payer or provider are at risk) for a specific period of time, dividing it by the average number of covered members or lives in that group during that period, and multiplying the result by 1,000. This indicator may be calculated for behavioral healthcare in aggregate, and/or by treatment modality (e.g., inpatient, residential, partial hospitalization, or outpatient treatment). A measure used to evaluate utilization management performance.

community rating: A premium rating methodology frequently used by HMOs. This is the rating methodology required of federally qualified HMOs and of HMOs under the laws of many states, and occasionally indemnity plans under certain circumstances. The HMO using this method must charge the same amount of money per member for all members of a plan. The methodology does not allow for employer account-specific variables to influence pricing. Contrasts with *experience rating.*

copayment: The fee or fixed payment charged to a member at the time of services for certain covered services and benefits. Copayments of $5 or $10 are common in the managed care industry. Practitioners and facilities are responsible for the collection of copayments from clients.

cost of living adjustment (COLA): Changes, i.e., increases, in the level of benefits provided under an income replacement or reimbursement program that are proportional to changes in a price index, such as the consumer price index (CPI).

cost of services (COS) ratio: The ratio between the cost incurred by the managed care entity that is directly related to service delivery and the amount of revenue acquired. A COS ratio of 80 percent or more is common in MBC operations, and excludes administrative and marketing costs as well as profit.

cost sharing: The apportioning of healthcare costs between a healthcare plan and individual participants through employee contributions, deductibles, and coinsurance.

cost shifting: The practice by some providers of redistributing the (negative) difference between normal charges and amounts received from certain payers by increasing charges made to other payers. For example, in order for a community hospital to provide free services to indigent patients, the facility might increase its charges to populations covered by commercial insurance payers.

current procedural terminology (CPT) codes: Sets of five-digit codes frequently used in claims submissions for billing professional services. Examples include 90801, diagnostic interview, 60 minutes; 90844, individual therapy, 45 minutes-50 minutes; and 90847, couples/family therapy, 60 minutes.

D **deductible:** The amount of money the policyholder must pay each year before insurance benefits begin. A deductible is generally associated with traditional indemnity insurance.

discounted fee-for-service: An agreed-upon rate for service between the provider and payer that is usually less than the provider's full fee. This amount may consist of a fixed amount per service or a percentage discount. Providers generally negotiate such financial arrangements because they represent a means to increase their volume or reduce the threat of losing patient volume to competitors. Employers and consumers benefit from these arrangements, as they create saving compared to full fee arrangements.

domestic partner coverage: Benefit coverage that recognizes the relationship between two unrelated people that is the approximate equivalent of marriage but that does not involve a formal marriage declaration. Domestic partnership is typically characterized by (1) intention of permanence, (2) long-term cohabitation, (3) shared finances, and (4) some public or documented commitment. Benefit plans that recognize domestic partnerships treat the partners of participants as if they were spouses. Domestic partners are also known as cohabitants or significant others.

E **electronic fund transfer (EFT):** The transfer of money between businesses and individuals by use of computer-generated debit and credit entries rather than with checks or cash.

enrolled group: Persons with the same employer or with membership in an organization who are enrolled collectively in a health plan or MCO.

enrollee: Any person eligible, as either a subscriber or a dependent, in an employee benefit plan. (Synonyms: beneficiary, eligible individual, member, participant.)

episode of care (EOC): An alternative from of healthcare financing where rates paid to a *provider* are established on an all-inclusive per-case basis. This type of financing has a built-in *stop loss*, where reimbursement for services revert to an established per diem rate after a certain number of days.

expenditure cap: A term becoming associated with the healthcare reform movement. It refers to a maximum amount that the government will pay for medical costs.

experience: A term used to describe the relationship of premium to claims for a plan, coverage, or benefits for a stated time period. Usually expressed as a percent or ratio. See also *medical loss ratio* (MLR).

experience rating: A premium rating methodology that adjusts to a customer's rate based on the utilization experience and other factors specific to the account. This system allows for lower premiums for employers who have healthy workforces, and contrasts with *community rating* methodology, which averages data for multiple groups of employees.

F **fee-for-service:** A traditional means of billing by healthcare providers for each service performed. Payments are in specific amounts for specific services rendered, covering either the entire service or just a portion of the service (as opposed to retainer, salary, or other contract arrangements). Both third-party payers and direct-pay patients are billed in this manner.

fee schedule: A listing of fees or allowances for specified medical or health procedures, which usually represents the maximum amounts the MCO or insurance plan will pay for specified procedures.

flat fee per case: A flat fee paid for a client's treatment based on his or her diagnosis and/or presenting problem. For this fee, the provider covers all of the services the client requires for a specific period of time.

*G*ross costs per 1,000: An indicator calculated by taking the gross costs incurred for services received by a specific group for a specific period of time, dividing it by the average number of covered members or lives in that group during the same period, and multiplying the result by 1,000. This is calculated for behavioral health care in the aggregate and by modality of treatment (e.g., inpatient, residential, partial hospitalization, and outpatient). This measure is used to evaluate utilization management performance. This is the key concept for the providers who are funded on a capitated basis. They must closely monitor this indicator, making sure to provide necessary care while controlling costs.

*H*CFA 1500: A form that is commonly used by professionals and facilities to bill payers for services. Originally the form was developed by HCFA for the billing of Medicare for services provided to its participants.

Health Care Financing Administration: A federal agency within the Department of Health and Human Services that administers the Medicare program.

I **incurred claims:** A financial method for evaluating a plan's history or performance. The incurred method reassigns financial liability from a plan year in which the claim was received or reported into the plan year from which the claim was generated (i.e., when the services were performed). Contrast to *paid claims.*

L **load:** The amount added to an insurance premium to cover administrative expenses, acquisition costs, taxes, contingency reserves, and profits.

loss ratio: The ratio of claims to premiums.

M **medical loss ratio (MLR):** The amount of revenues from health insurance premiums that is used to pay for the medical services covered by the plan. Usually referred to by a ratio, such as 0.95, which means that 95 percent of premiums were used to purchase medical services. The goal is to keep this ratio below 1.00—preferably in the 0.80-0.85 range.

medical reimbursement account: An increasingly popular feature of new employer-sponsored health benefit plans designed to assist employees with the increased cost sharing associated with these plans. The employee annually sets aside pretax dollars in the medical reimbursement account that may be used for expenses such as copayments, deductibles, eyeglasses, well-baby care, or child care expenses. Employers sometimes contribute to or match employee contributions to these accounts.

Medicare adjusted average per capita cost: The actuarial estimate made by *HCFA (Health Care Financing Administration)* for Part A and Part B cost of providing *Medicare*-covered services in a given area. Based on the fee-for-service sector, this rate is set by county, age, and sex, adjusted for each given period.

member payment: Fees or payments that the member is responsible for providing, including plan *deductibles, coinsurance,* and *copayments.*

morbidity: An actuarial concept applied to setting health and disability insurance rates that shows the average incidence of illness occurring in a large group of people.

mortality: An actuarial concept applied to setting life and disability insurance rates that shows the average death rates for a large group of people.

O **out-of-pocket maximum:** The maximum amount an insured person will have to pay for a covered healthcare expense. Often this amount is $500, $1,000, or a percentage of an insured person's annual salary. The amount is usually calculated on a yearly basis.

P **paid claims:** A financial method of measuring a plan's performance or history. Paid claims views a liability as belonging to the plan exclusively for the plan year in which the claim is paid, regardless of when the service was performed.

PCP capitation: A reimbursement system for healthcare providers of primary care services who receive a prepayment every month. The payment amount is based on age, sex, and benefit plan of every member assigned to that physician for that month. Specialty capitation plans also exist but are not as widely used. When payments to specialists are also capitated, a subcapitation system results. Initially shunned by many physicians, these arrangements are increasingly the major revenue source for primary care doctors. Such arrangements are an emerging method of payment for behavioral care professionals.

per diem reimbursement: A system used most commonly with hospitals or partial hospital programs and based on a predetermined set rate per day of care, rather than usual charges. This system is a cost-containment measure that usually assures volume referrals for the facility and also assures discounted fees for the managed care entity.

per employee per year (PEPY): A payment method used in financing employee assistance programs on a prepaid, per capita basis. Such fees vary depending on services offered, but rates commonly range from $15 PEPY to $25 PEPY.

per member per month (PMPM): A payment method used in financing managed care arrangements under which the vendor is paid for each enrollee each month.

prospective rating: The setting of insurance rates for a defined future coverage period, such as one or two years, based upon that group's or a similar group's prior claims incurred history.

provider contract: A legal written agreement between a licensed healthcare facility, physician, or other healthcare provider and a health plan.

provider payment: Payment methods used by health plans to pay providers. Includes fee-for-service payments and capitation.

 **reasonable and customary charge:** Also known as usual, customary, and reasonable charge (UCR). The maximum amount an insurer will consider as eligible for reimbursement. A claims cost-control device.

reserves: Amounts set aside by insurers to ensure adequate funds to meet incurred but not reported future claims, extension of benefit claims, and expenses.

retention: The portion of an insurance premium allocated to expenses and profit.

retrospective rating: The determination of insurance rates at the end of the coverage period based on actual plan experience for that period. Retrospective rates are usually subject to a preset minimum and maximum.

risk management: The assumption of financial and/or legal responsibility of medical or behavioral healthcare.

risk sharing: A method by which medical insurance premiums are shared by plan sponsors and participants. This arrangement contrasts with traditional indemnity plans in which insurance premiums belong solely to insurance companies that assume all risk of using these premiums. Risk-sharing arrangements are increasingly common in all fields of healthcare and involve purchasers (in ASO arrangements), MCOs, facilities, group practices, PHOs, and individual providers.

S **self-insurance:** A program for providing group insurance with benefits financed entirely through the internal means of the policyholder, as opposed to purchasing coverage from commercial carriers. This plan is exempt from the *Employee Retirement Income Security Act of 1974 (ERISA)* and from most regulation. Thus, mostly large employers use it.

stop loss: The predetermined dollar limit (usually in connection with a catastrophic claim) that limits a member's out-of-pocket expenses. Under certain contracts, it can also be applied to maximum dollar responsibility of an insurance company.

subcapitation: A financial arrangement that exists when an organization being paid under a capitated system contracts with other entities on a capitated basis, sharing a portion of the original capitated premium. For example, when an **HMO** *carves out* behavioral care benefits to a behavioral care company, the specialty company is subcapitated and at risk for the provision of the mental health/substance abuse benefits. Such organizations may then further subcapitate providers of facilities, thus extending the risk-sharing arrangement.

subrogation: The act of recovering moneys from any third-party payer when expenses incurred could result in possible legal action.

T **tolerable loss ratio (TLR):** The loss ratio the insurer can fund without losing money on the group.

 **unbundling:** A form of *code gaming* where each step of a medical procedure is billed as a separate item.

upcoding: A form of *code gaming* also known as code creep, where a medical procedure is redefined so that it falls into a billing category which qualifies for a higher reimbursement.

_W_withhold pool: The amount withheld from a PCP's capitation payment or a specialist's payment amount to cover expenditures greater than budgeted or expected in serving a specified enrollee group. If utilization is less than the withhold pool, or if the pool remains relatively unused, specialists get some portion of that pool back as payment. Such withhold provisions are common, but controversial in the HMO industry, as critics maintain that they incentivize the withholding of services to patients for the financial gain of practitioners.

Practice Management
Terms and Concepts

A **acceptability:** This term refers to the "fit" of the practitioner, program, or service with the member who is receiving care. The term reflects an organization's *cultural competence*, or its capability to assess and meet the special cultural, ethnic, and communicative needs and preferences of its enrolled members. The term also indicates the level of *customer satisfaction* with the quality and accessibility of healthcare services.

accessibility: A member's ability to obtain medical or behavioral care. Accessibility takes into consideration the *availability* of services, their *acceptability* to the member, the location of the services, the availability of convenient transportation, the hours of operation of the services, the cost of care (such as *copayments* or *deductibles*), and other factors. For example, although enough appointment slots are available to the member, if the member cannot get through to the organization on the telephone in order to schedule an appointment, the appointments are not accessible.

accountability: The responsibility of an organization, department, or individual for achieving defined goals.

accountable health plan (AHP): A regional or geographic joint venture between practitioners and institutions (such as insurance companies, HMOs, or hospitals) that would assume responsibility and risk for delivering medical care to a specific population or group. Physicians and other providers would either own, work for, or contract with these health plans. Often referred to as community care network (CCN), organized system of care, integrated delivery system (IDS), or integrated health delivery system (IHDS). Also known as community accountable healthcare networks (CAHNs) or health purchasing alliances (HPAs).

adverse selection: This type of selection occurs when a health plan enrolls members who are not as healthy as the general population. Such members tend to use medical or behavioral care services at higher rates than other members of the health plan or the general population. Thus adverse selection increases the cost of providing services and may ultimately result in higher prices to consumers.

alternate delivery: Health services that are provided in settings other than inpatient, acute-care hospitals but which provide treatment plans for conditions that were traditionally treated primarily in these settings. Skilled and intermediary nursing facilities, hospice programs, and home healthcare are examples of alternate health service delivery settings. Behavioral care examples include ambulatory detoxification services, partial hospitalization programs, and in-home therapy or crisis intervention services. Alternate delivery systems are designed to provide needed services in a more cost-effective manner and are proliferating in managed care environments.

alternative healthcare: Any of a wide array of healthcare services and interventions viewed as alternatives to traditional allopathic medicine. This growing area of healthcare includes interventions from treatment systems such as acupuncture, chiropractic, homeopathy, naturopathy, and many others. An increasing number of health plans, in response to consumer interest and the emerging body of empirical data supporting the efficacy of these services, cover some alternative healthcare services.

ambulatory surgical center: A facility that provides surgical services that do not require a hospital stay.

ancillary care: Diagnostic and/or supportive services.

ancillary provider: The term for any nonphysician provider that provides supplementary care. Some examples of ancillary providers are laboratories, physical therapists, and pharmacists.

ancillary services: Services received in an inpatient hospital setting other than room, board, and nursing services. For example, bandages, prescriptions, and lab services are usually considered ancillary services. Managed care contracts typically include all charges for such services as a part of an overall daily fee.

assessment and referral: An *employee assistance program* (EAP) model in which clinical services are offered with the objective of assessing the presenting problem of the employee or family member and referring the client to an appropriate treatment or other resource for problem resolution. Such models typically allow up to three visits for the professional to conduct this function. Contrasts with *short-term counseling* EAP model.

attestation: A signed statement by the attending physician affirming the fact that the stated principal and secondary diagnoses and procedures identified for a specific case accurately reflect the status and care to a member.

authorization: Written approval issued by the health plan or *primary care physician* (PCP) for specific services that indicate prior knowledge of the services to be rendered. An authorization does not necessarily guarantee payment of all or part of the claim.

availability: The extent to which certain types of services and programs are available to or obtainable by members of health plans in defined locations.

average length of stay (ALOS): A statistic calculated for identified parameters that reflects an average hospitalization period for similar cases, groups, etc. This term may also be applied to behavioral care services, including outpatient care. To determine the ALOS, divide the total number of patients utilizing a particular service, such as inpatient bed days, into the total number of bed days used in a defined time period. The result is that population's ALOS. For example: 100 patients used a total of 500 bed days in a particular period; 500 divided by 100 equals 5 days for the group's ALOS. The monitoring and trending of a population's ALOS for any service is a routine function in managed care systems due to its clinical, quality, and financial implications for the service delivery system.

B **beneficiary:** An individual eligible for benefits from a specified program.

benefit period: A period of time, usually a calendar year, over which healthcare benefits are payable. Also pertains to a time period in which a benefits deductible may be met or to an accumulation period.

broker: A licensed insurance professional who represents purchasers such as employers or labor organizations in acquiring insurance products and coverage.

C **calendar year deductible:** A *deductible* that recurs and must be met again each year.

Canadian healthcare model: A system of healthcare in which there are no insurance companies; instead, healthcare is financed through taxation and administered by the Canadian federal government. Those in the United States who view a public healthcare system as advantageous or superior often advocate for this system.

case mix: The relative frequency and intensity of hospital admissions or services reflecting different needs and uses of hospital resources. Case mix can be measured based on patients' diagnoses or the severity of their illnesses, the utilization of services, or the characteristics of the hospital.

centers of excellence: Medical or treatment facilities considered to be outstanding in the advanced level of care offered for a disease or delivery of a specific procedure. Customers of health plans or behavioral care delivery systems sometimes mandate the inclusion of centers of excellence in networks. Such delivery systems also use centers of excellence as a part of their marketing and competitive efforts.

clinic without walls (CWW): Similar to an *independent practice association*, this type of physician or provider grouping represents a legal and formal entity. Under such arrangements, the legal entity provides administrative and support services to each physician/provider, and the provider continues to practice in his/her own facility. The provided services can include marketing, billing, collection, or staffing.

clinical or critical pathways: A map or guide of preferred treatment/intervention activities. Clinical or critical pathways outline the types of information needed to make decisions, the timelines for applying that information, and what action needs to be taken by whom. These pathways can provide a way to monitor care in real time. These pathways are developed by clinicians for specific diseases or events.

clinical decision support: The capability of an information system to provide key data to physicians, mental health professionals, and other clinicians to assist them in achieving better outcomes and in offering standardized treatment plans based on best practices. These systems can also alert case managers that a client's eligibility or benefits for a service is about to be exhausted. Clinical decision support is a key functional requirement to support *clinical or critical pathways.*

closed panel health plan: A program that requires participants to utilize professionals, pharmacies, and facilities from a list of providers with which it has established a contracted relationship.

comprehensive outpatient rehabilitation facility: A facility that offers full rehabilitative programs, including physicians' services, physical, speech, occupational, and respiratory therapies, counseling, and other related services.

consumer/member/customer services: These terms refer to the administrative systems that enroll the customer, provide information about how to access and use the organization, handle consumer concerns, and assist the consumer in receiving clinical services. Examples include, but are not limited to: enrollment, claims services, appointments, and telephone systems.

contract: Refers to the legal agreement between an HMO and a provider or between the HMO and an employer.

contracted healthcare facility: Any facility other than a hospital that is operated by or has an agreement with a specific HMO or health plan to render services to subscribers.

contracted health professional: An individual who is licensed or otherwise authorized to deliver medical services, and who has an agreement with an HMO or a health plan to render services to subscribers.

coordination of benefits: Arrangement among insurance carriers to avoid duplication of payment when an individual is covered by more than one insurance plan. Commonly referred to as COB, this claims payment function follows strict protocols concerning primary and secondary payment responsibilities when multiple payers are involved in providing coverage.

cost outlier: A case that does not exceed the length of stay criteria for the *day outlier,* but whose charges (adjusted to cost) exceed the threshold for a specific diagnostic-related group (DRG).

cultural competence: An organization's ability to ensure that provider panels or networks reflect the racial, ethnic, cultural, linguistic, and other diverse characteristics of the member population or workforce, including language proficiency whenever possible.

D **day outlier:** A case in which the number of inpatient days in a hospital or other stay exceeds the average length of stay for discharges in the *diagnostic-related group* (DRG) by a fixed number of days.

deductible: An amount the covered individual must pay to providers or facilities before an insurance product or plan begins reimbursement for covered expenses.

dental maintenance organization (DMO): An organization providing comprehensive dental services for a fixed premium, generally per person. In design, DMOs are the same as HMOs, each providing its own type of services.

direct contracting: A method of providing healthcare services to a specific population by a provider or group of providers through contracting directly with an employer or labor organization payer, thus eliminating the third-party insurance carrier.

disease management: A type of product or service often offered by pharmaceutical companies aimed at effective management of the health of a given population. This product or service combines the use of patient health screening technology, physician and allied health professionals' education, and accessability to large databases created by the pharmaceutical companies to predict those patients at risk for various illnesses. Thus, early intervention and treatment in a cost-efficient manner can be provided while creating opportunities for targeted prevention initiatives.

disenrollment: The process of ending membership from a health plan. Disenrollment can occur voluntarily or for cause and is typically initiated by a health plan or an employer-customer of the health plan. Procedures for this process are defined in members' contracts and statements of members' rights and are often defined in regulatory processes as well.

Drug-Free Workplace Act: A 1993 federal statute requiring employers with $25,000 or more in federal government contracts to certify they are maintaining a drug-free workplace. One of the impacts of this act was the proliferation of employee assistance programs as a tool to document employers' efforts to achieve the ambitious objective enunciated in the law's title.

dual choice: The federal requirement that, upon request, certain employers must offer a *federally qualified HMO* as an alternative to its conventional health plan. Some states have similar dual choice requirements.

Employee Retirement Income Security Act of 1974 (ERISA): Also called the Pension Reform Act, this act regulates the majority of private pension and welfare group benefit plans in the United States. This act sets forth requirements governing, among many areas, participation, crediting of service, vesting, communication and disclosure, funding, and fiduciary conduct. It requires that insurance plans be established pursuant to a written instrument that describes the benefits provided under the plan, names the persons responsible for the operation of the plan, and spells out the arrangements for funding and amending the plan.

employment assistance program (EAP): An employer-sponsored counseling and consultation service aimed at assisting employees or their family members who are experiencing emotional, substance abuse, family, or other problems that can interfere with productivity or worker safety. EAPs provide employers with a workplace-based tool for prevention and early intervention activities. The EAP may be voluntary or mandatory. In mandatory EAPs, the benefit plan only reimburses care that is delivered through a system that is accessed through an EAP assessor. Incentivized EAPs feature a higher level of reimbursement when a member of the EAP provider network renders care. In addition to provider networks, EAPs may also offer utilization management and other managed care functions. Core services of EAPs include assessment, referral, manager/supervisor consultation, wellness and other employee educational and informational services, and critical incidence response interventions. Some EAP models offer telephonic counseling, short-term counseling services, and quality management services. EAPs save employers money through increased productivity of the workforce and reduced absenteeism, job-related injuries, and disabilities, as well as recruitment and training costs. They are also helpful to employers in avoiding wrongful discharge litigation.

enrollment period: A specified time period provided by an employer and a healthcare organization during which employees may select a healthcare benefit plan or a particular offering from within a plan. Selection may be done in person or electronically, and may be based on literature distributed by the vendors or through information obtained in meetings conducted by vendor representatives.

evidence of insurability: A personal description that lists factors regarding a person's physical condition, medical history, and other information upon which an insurer could base an underwriting decision. Although evidence of insurability is required for individual insurance coverage, it is seldom required for group policies other than very small ones.

exclusion: Items or services that are not a benefit of a specified plan or program.

exclusive provider organization (EPO): A type of provider organization similar to an HMO. Such entities often use PCPs as gatekeepers, often capitate providers, have a limited provider panel, and use an authorization system. These entities are exclusive because members must remain within the defined network to receive benefit coverage.

expected claim: The claims forecast for a group or covered member. The expected claim level becomes the break-even point with respect to the expected premium for a period of coverage.

Federal Insurance Contribution Act (FICA): A federal act establishing the tax taken from employees and matched by the employer, or paid entirely by the self-employed worker, that pays for *Medicare* Part A insurance after age sixty-five or with other qualifying diagnoses. FICA taxes were first collected in 1937.

federal qualification: The federal seal of approval for HMOs based on a review of such things as the HMO's organization, delivery system, and benefit coverages.

fiduciary: Under *ERISA*, any person or entity that exercises discretionary control over the administration of a benefit plan. Self-insured employers can delegate this responsibility to managed care organizations or utilization review organizations.

flexcare: A healthcare product that combines the use of a traditional *fee-for-service* (FFS) plan and managed healthcare network options.

formulary: A list of drug products and, in some instances, dosage forms approved for coverage under the health plan. The formulary is subject to periodic review and modification.

G **gatekeeper:** An individual, usually a clinician, who controls the access to healthcare services for members of a specific group. In many HMO settings, this gatekeeper is the *primary care physician* (PCP). In other healthcare delivery systems (and in HMOs in which behavioral health services are contracted out), the gatekeeper is often a case manager.

group: Number of persons from one employer or other source who have selected or have the same insurance benefits, and who are thereafter identified by an assigned group number.

group model HMO: In this service delivery model, an HMO contracts with a medical group (such as one or more physician group practices that are not owned by the HMO) for the provision of healthcare services. The relationship between the HMO and the medical group is generally very close, although there are wide variations in the relative independence of the group from the HMO. The HMO does not own the practices. The HMO pays the groups at a negotiated rate, and each group is responsible for paying its doctors and other staff and for paying for hospital care or care from outside specialists. This is a form of *closed panel health plan.*

group service agreement: The legal contract between the employer, or individual, and the insurance company. The GSA is filed with and approved by the Bureau of Insurance or other regulatory entities.

H **health maintenance organization (HMO):** A highly regulated delivery system that provides comprehensive healthcare in return for a preset monthly payment (e.g., per member per month). The definition has two key components: a health plan that places at least some of the providers at risk for medical expenses and a health plan that utilizes *primary care physicians* (PCPs) as *gatekeepers* (although some HMOs do not). Obtaining care without a primary care physician's *referral* or obtaining care from a non-*network* member usually results in less or no payment for services by the payer organization. HMOs may be operated on a nonprofit basis or as for-profit businesses, and their customers include companies, labor organizations, and governmental employers. Spurred by federal legislation during the 1970s, HMOs have become a common healthcare delivery model, as they are seen as a viable means of correcting inflationary and structural problems in the traditional healthcare system in the United States.

health risk appraisal (HRA): A survey used by employers to estimate the likelihood of an insured employee experiencing death, illness, or injury in the future. It helps employers decide whether wellness and other preventive care programs are necessary.

healthcare prepayment plan: A contract with *Medicare* to provide Medicare Part B services to beneficiaries on a fee-for-service arrangement. A *premium* is charged to cover the 20 percent nonreimbursement cost.

HMO Act of 1973: Amended in 1988, this historic and influential law allowed HMOs to become *federally qualified* by meeting various standards. Once so designated, the HMO has the right to ask any local employer of twenty-five or more employees to offer its services as a healthcare benefit option. HMOs were required to charge the same "community rate" to all employers, pooling all employers together for risk purposes. HMOs were allowed to adjust premiums by actual employer group experience, no longer adhering to a community rating system. Caps were placed on charges to smaller employer groups. HMOs were also permitted to provide services through non-HMO physicians, charging extra fees when members utilized such services.

home health agency: A certified agency that provides intermittent skilled nursing services and other therapeutic services in the home when such services are *medically necessary* and when the patient is confined to the home.

hospice: An organization or agency that is primarily engaged in providing pain relief, symptom management, and supportive services to terminally ill patients and their families.

hospital: An institution that provides inpatient, outpatient, emergency, diagnostic, and therapeutic services.

*I*ncurred but not reimbursed (IBNR): Refers to claims which reflect clinical services already delivered but, for whatever reason, have not yet been reimbursed to the professional or facility.

independent physician association; individual practice association; independent provider association (IPAs): Organizations that are typically formed and operated by physicians and marketed to employers. Individual private practice physicians are paid either a fee or a fixed amount per patient to take care of the members. Under this arrangement, physicians still see their individual patients, as well as patients from the HMO. This model also includes entities that contract with groups of providers, including corporate providers such as behavioral health centers. Each provider agrees to see patients/clients from plans that contract with the HMO of which the IPA is a part and to serve these clients for agreed-upon fees. Such IPAs often are not associated with a single HMO, but serve a number of them under contract. This is frequently the case in specialty services such as behavioral healthcare.

integrated behavioral healthcare: Refers to the combination of independent managed care services into a seamless delivery system for behavioral health concerns. Components may include *employee assistance programs*, a telephone counseling *triage, utilization management*, behavioral treatment *networks*, claims payment, data management, *quality management*, treatment outcomes studies, and access to *primary care* delivery systems.

integrated health plans: A type of benefit plan in which all employees are enrolled into a single managed care system for all healthcare services, be they medical, dental, or behavioral. Members may have options to choose non-network providers, but at an increased cost.

intermediary: A knowledgeable benefits professional, such as a benefits consultant, who assists plan sponsors in designing, purchasing, and administering health insurance programs.

***International Classification of Diseases, 9th Revision, Clinical Modification* (ICD-9-CM):** A compilation of numeric codes used to identify and code illnesses, conditions, and symptoms.

*M*anaged care or managed behavioral care (MBC): Refers to any of a variety of systems and strategies aimed at marshaling appropriate clinical and financial resources to ensure needed care for consumers. It features increased accountability for providers, the overall coordination of care, the elimination of duplicative or unnecessary services, and the overall improvement of the quality and outcomes of treatment services.

managed care organization (MCO): A term that describes any HMO or managed behavioral care entity.

managed healthcare: A broad term referencing a range of systems such as HMOs, PPOs, or behavioral healthcare networks that use financial incentives and management controls to direct patients to providers who are responsible for giving appropriate care in cost-effective treatment settings. Such systems evolved from the market need during the 1970s to provide a means of controlling the inflationary trends in healthcare, and later in behavioral healthcare, as well as correcting other structural problems in the U.S. healthcare system. This term is often used as an industry label.

management information system (MIS): The computer hardware, software, and automated systems that provide support for the management of a business.

management (or medical) services organization (MSO): An entity formed by, for example, a hospital, a group of physicians, or an independent entity to provide business-related services such as marketing and data collection to a grouping of providers such as an IPA, PHO, or CWW.

mandated benefits: Minimal benefit levels established by statutes enacted by state legislatures. These vary from state to state and can add to overall healthcare costs. *ERISA* exempts employers who are self-insured from these mandates. Other exceptions have been made for "basic," low-cost insurance products that can be offered to the uninsured segment of the workforce.

mandated offering: Similar to a mandated benefit, except that instead of being a requirement in each policy, the coverage need only be offered to a member, who is not required to buy it.

mandated providers: Healthcare providers, typically *ancillary providers*, whose services, under state law, must be covered by an insurance policy. Examples include: psychologists, clinical social workers, podiatrists, and chiropractors.

Medicaid: A federal program that provides medical benefits for certain low-income or needy persons according to various cash grant categories and authorized by Title XIX of the Social Security Act.

medically necessary: Term used to describe services or supplies that are appropriate and necessary for the symptoms, diagnosis, or treatment of a medical condition. Medically necessary services are provided for the diagnosis or direct care and treatment of the medical condition. They meet the standards of good medical practice within the medical community in the service area. They are not primarily for the convenience of the plan member or a plan provider but are the most appropriate level of care or supply of service that can safely be provided to treat a condition. Many health plans do not provide full benefit coverage for services that are elective in nature rather than being medically necessary.

Medicare: Title XVIII of the Social Security Act of 1965, which provides payment for medical and health services to the population aged sixty-five and older regardless of income, certain disabled persons, and persons with end stage renal disease (ESRD). The major benefits include physician services, hospital care, home care, dialysis, and extended care facility coverage for a definitive period of time, for example, up to 100 days per calendar year for skilled nursing care. Medicare Part A is hospital insurance provided by Medicare that can help pay for inpatient hospital care, medically necessary inpatient care in a skilled nursing facility, home healthcare and hospice care, and ESRD treatment. Medicare Part B is a Medicare administered insurance that helps pay for certain medically necessary practitioner services, outpatient hospital services, and supplies not covered by Part A. Doctors' services are covered under Part B, even if they are provided to a patient in an inpatient setting. Part B can also pay for some home health services when the beneficiary does not qualify for part A.

Medicare secondary payer: A Medicare determination in which participation is limited to coinsurance status because the member is eligible for primary coverage from another source, such as automobile insurance or worker's compensation, or when a beneficiary is employed and covered under employer health insurance.

Medigap: Medicare supplemental insurance that pays for the annual deductible and the 20 percent copayment required "out-of-pocket."

member: An individual who is eligible for benefits under a healthcare plan, particularly an HMO or other prepaid system.

mental health services: A wide range of diagnostic, therapeutic, and rehabilitative services used in the treatment of mental health/ substance abuse disorders.

mixed model HMO: A health plan that includes more than one form of HMO within a single plan. For example, a staff model HMO might also contract with independent physician groups or with individual private practice physicians.

multiple employer trust (MET): A legal trust established by a plan sponsor that brings together a number of small, unrelated employers for the purpose of providing group medical coverage on an insured or self-funded basis.

National Practitioner Data Bank (NPDB): A federally mandated agency that is the repository of information about settled malpractice suits and adverse acts, sanctions, or restrictions against the practice privileges of a physician.

network or provider network: A group of providers that is organized, accredited, and administered by a managed care company. Members of the network agree to practice in an effective, cost-conscious manner, utilizing the managed care firm's clinical guidelines or standards. Members of the network also agree to a discounted fee arrangement. In turn, they are eligible for referrals through the managed care firm or through members of employer groups contracting with the firm. Network providers agree to the managed care firm's quality management program. The network may include both inpatient and outpatient providers. It is increasingly important for providers to join networks in order to allow access to their services by large numbers of potential patients. Success in such networks has increasingly required providers to become familiar with effective and efficient therapies and modalities, to manage practices efficiently, and to develop innovative services in order to compete successfully for referrals.

network model: A health plan that contracts with multiple physician groups or other providers to deliver healthcare to members. Generally limited to large single or multispecialty groups.

A network model is different from a group model plan that contracts with a single medical group. A network model is different from an IPA that contracts through an intermediary. A network model is also different from a direct contract plan that contracts with individual physicians in the community. Many current behavioral healthcare networking efforts are attempts to create service systems along this line or to integrate behavioral healthcare practices into such entities.

O **open enrollment period:** The time period during which an employee may change or join a healthcare plan. This usually occurs once per year for each employer group, typically during the fall. Open enrollment is a period of intense promotion aimed at prospective members by competing healthcare plans.

outlier: A case where the length of stay or cost of care exceeds the cutoff or threshold for a specific *diagnostic-related group* (DRG). See *outlier review.*

outlier reviews:

- **cost outlier review:** A required review. This review is also to determine whether the services billed were *medically necessary,* were performed at an appropriate *level of care,* were not billed more than once, were actually rendered, and were ordered by a physician.

- **day outlier review:** A required review. This review also determines *appropriateness* of *level of care* for all hospital days.

- **peer review:** The formal assessment by members of the same profession.

out-of-area benefits: Benefits supplied by a plan to its subscribers or enrollees when they need services outside the geographic limits of the HMO. These benefits usually include emergency care benefits, plus low fee-for-service payments for nonemergency care.

out-of-area provider: A provider that is not contracted with a member's HMO and does not practice in the same geographical area as outlined in the HMO member's agreement.

out-of-network services: Refers to services received through professionals or facilities not affiliated with the network of approved professionals and facilities. This term may also pertain to services rendered by network resources when they are delivered without preauthorization by the MCO in nonemergency situations. In this scenario, the provider or the member may be responsible for some or all of the cost of these services according to the member's contract. Increasingly, MCOs are offering products that allow members, at the point of service, to choose a non-network provider and still receive benefit coverage.

P **partial hospitalization program:** A behavioral healthcare setting that provides an interdisciplinary program of medical and therapeutic services at least three hours per day, five days per week. Partial hospitalization programs may be either free standing or part of a broader behavioral healthcare or medical system.

physician-hospital organization: An emerging variety of business arrangements among physicians and hospital(s) wherein a single entity (the PHO) agrees to provide services to insurers' subscribers for one price. Formerly called a MeSH or medical staff-hospital organization. Often superseded by a medical foundation, which carries out a similar role but which is more integrated in its governance and operation.

point-of-care technology: Those technologies that enable physicians and other clinicians to electronically record findings, enter orders, and review information from the location at which care is provided. Input from clinicians directly changes the databases.

point-of-service (POS) plan: A type of benefit plan in which the insured person can choose to receive services either from participating providers or from providers outside the MCO's network. This type of plan offers consumers more flexibility, more coverage, and more access to specialists without referrals from PCPs. In-network care is more fully covered. Members may choose to use a nonparticipating provider at a reduced coverage level and with more out-of-pocket cost (similar to more traditional indemnity health insurance). Such POS plans combine both HMO-like systems with indemnity systems. Often known as open-ended HMOs or PPOs, these plans permit insured members to choose providers outside the plan, yet are designed to encourage the use of network providers. Behavioral care systems offer similar benefit programs.

position papers: A collection of papers that states the current position of an HMO on new, experimental, or controversial procedures or on the treatment of specific conditions. These often indicate whether or not a procedure would be included in the insurance benefits.

predetermination: An administrative procedure whereby a health-care provider submits a treatment plan to a third party before treatment is initiated. The third party usually reviews the treatment plan, monitoring one or more of the following: patient's eligibility, covered service, amounts payable, application of appropriate deductibles, and copayment factors and maximums. Under some programs, for instance, predetermination by the third party is required when covered charges are expected to exceed a certain amount.

preferred provider arrangement (PPA): An agreement between a business entity and a provider or group of providers (a *network*). Differs from *a preferred provider organization* (PPO), which is an actual organization.

preferred provider organization (PPO): A variation of traditional fee-for-service care arrangements. An arrangement by which an entity contracts with an organization of providers (a network of physicians, dentists, and/or hospitals and other practitioners) for specified services. These services are delivered on a discounted fee basis, and the providers are guaranteed a volume of referrals, prompt claims payments, etc. The providers also agree to comply with utilization management procedures. PPO members get better benefits (greater coverage) when they use the PPO's network and pay higher out-of-pocket costs when they receive care outside the PPO network. In addition, PPOs generally use primary care physicians to ensure that hospitalization occurs only when absolutely necessary, with extensive concurrent utilization review.

prepaid group practice plan: A plan under which contractually specified health services are rendered by participating physicians to an enrolled group of persons, with a fixed periodic payment in advance made by or on behalf of each person or family.

preprocedure review: Also known as preprocedure certification, the review and determination of the reasonableness, medical necessity, and appropriateness of hospitalization made prior to a member's admission.

primary care physician (PCP): Usually internists, family physicians, general practitioners, and pediatricians who perform the key role of the overall provision of care and maintenance of health for defined subsets of HMO members. Most HMOs require members to choose a primary care physician from that entity's network who then provides (or authorizes referrals to specialty physicians or facilities) all care for that member. Some managed care plans require PCP screening and referral of members in need of mental health or substance abuse treatment services as well. PCPs are typically compensated for services through a capitation arrangement, are subject to quality review and oversight processes, and participate in the clinical and administrative management of the HMO.

professional liability: Refers to the risk assumed by practitioners for improper or negligent treatment of a patient resulting in damage or injury to the patient. A function of MCOs is to review the litigation records of network providers as a quality assurance measure. MCOs require a professional liability insurance coverage as a basic requirement of doing business as a network-affiliated practitioner.

profile: Aggregated data in formats that display patterns of healthcare services over a defined period of time.

profile analysis: Review and analysis of profiles to identify and assess patterns of healthcare services.

provider: A commonly used term referencing a professional who delivers clinical services to a managed care member. A *facility provider* refers to hospitals or other institutional entities.

provider analytical tools: Software programs that aggregate provider practice information and report along any number of dimensions, including length of treatment episode, diagnostic patterns, patient satisfaction with the professional's services, and treatment outcomes. MCOs profile their provider networks to ensure that they are efficient, effective, and meet minimum standards for patient satisfaction and quality. These tools are used to evaluate the overall performance of a network of providers or an individual provider or facility. Most MCOs share such profile information with network providers partially as a means of shaping providers' treatment and service delivery patterns.

provider level classification: A system used by managed care companies to categorize network providers along certain characteristics of importance to the MCO or consumers. These classification systems are often used to indicate whether the provider is fully contracted, has been used only on a noncontracted basis (and therefore not accountable to a range of quality assurance and other protocols applicable to contracted providers), or to categorize the providers' understanding of and compliance with the key functions related to providing effective and efficient treatment. The provider level classification may help determine the amount of oversight or intensity of management a provider receives from the managed care company as well as the volume of referrals. This classification is usually one part of an integrated provider database available to intake and care management staff of MCOs that also includes service specialty and other key practice information.

provider organization: A practice, clinic, mental health center, hospital, or other organization that is employed by managed health programs to provide treatment services.

provider profiling: Statistical comparisons of a physician or other professional's practice patterns regarding such factors as numbers of visits, numbers of referrals, and numbers of laboratory tests. The statistics are used to develop norms for identifying the most and least efficient providers.

provider relations manager: An important coordinating position found in most MCOs that has responsibility for the recruitment, contracting, credentialing, orientation, training, and ongoing management of providers and facilities. Provider relations is a function in all managed care systems that utilize provider networks (as opposed to staff models).

S **second opinion:** Requirement of some health plans to obtain an opinion about the *medical necessity* and *appropriateness* of proposed services by a practitioner, in addition to the one originally making the decision.

service area: The geographic area within which an HMO is authorized to provide services, and where a person must live to be able to become or remain a member of that HMO.

short-term counseling: An EAP model that has as a clinical objective the provision of counseling services to resolve many presenting problems of employees or their family members. Such models often allow up to five, six, or eight visits to achieve this objective. The short-term counseling model contrasts with the *assessment and referral* model EAP. The short-term counseling model can be as much as 50 percent more expensive for employers to provide in comparison with the assessment and referral model. It is usually utilized when the employer wishes to supplement the company-sponsored behavioral healthcare program with additional counseling services.

staff management program: A structured mechanism that at a minimum credentials, recredentials, orients, trains, monitors, supervises, and evaluates the qualifications and performance of clinical and nonclinical MCO staff and consultants involved at all levels of review activity.

staff model HMO: A type of HMO in which the doctors and other medical professionals are salaried employees of the HMO, and the HMO owns the clinics or healthcare centers in which they practice. Behavioral MCOs also may employ staff models or mixed staff models, as well as network delivery system models.

standards: Professionally developed criteria that provide a range of acceptable performance or outcome.

T **temporary absence:** Absence from the service area of ninety days or less. If a member travels and does not intend to return to the health plan service area within ninety days, it is considered a permanent move.

third-party administrator (TPA): Usually an out-of-house professional firm providing administrative services, such as paying claims, collecting premiums, and carrying out other administrative support services for employee benefit plans. (Synonyms: administrative agent, carrier, insurer, underwriter.)

total and permanent disability: Medical conditions that would allow continuation of coverage after its normal termination date.

W **working day:** Any of the days upon which necessary utilization management personnel are available to perform reviews and includes, at a minimum, Monday through Friday of every calendar week, except for observed holidays.

Quality Management
and Utilization Review
Terms and Concepts

A **accreditation:** A recognized evaluation that health care purchasers, regulators, and consumers can use to assess managed care plans. Accreditation provides an evaluation of how well a health plan manages all parts of its delivery system in order to improve healthcare for its members, and may be done by a professional society, a nongovernmental body, or a governmental agency. Accreditation is usually accomplished through on- and off-site evaluations conducted by a team of physicians and managed care experts. Accreditation provides reassurance and a sanction that a particular program, organization, or agency has met a stringent set of criteria.

admission review: Review of a member's medical record in order to determine whether a member's admission to an inpatient facility was reasonable and *medically necessary*, and whether the services were delivered in the most appropriate setting and *level of care*. Usually, the utilization review staff performs an admission review within twenty-four hours or on the first working day following the member's admission to a facility.

appeal: A formal request, by either a practitioner or a health plan member for reconsideration of a decision such as a utilization review recommendation, a benefit payment, an administrative action, or a quality of care or service issue. The goal of an appeal is the finding of a mutually acceptable solution. The formal process that a practitioner or a member can use to request the reconsideration is known as the appeals mechanism.

appropriateness of care: The suitability of care provided to a member given that member's healthcare needs. Appropriateness relates to whether an individual in need of certain hospital services actually received those services and, conversely, whether an individual had services ordered unnecessarily. Appropriate care must also be provided in the setting best suited to the member's needs given the current state of knowledge. Appropriateness of care criteria may vary among individual health plans.

B **benchmark:** Refers to the industry measure of best performance for a particular indicator or performance goal. The benchmarking process identifies the best performance in the industry (healthcare, behavioral care, or other industry) for a particular process or outcome, determines how that performance is achieved, and applies the lessons learned to improve performance.

Board of Health Professions: A state agency that issues licenses to medical and behavioral healthcare professionals such as physicians, nurses, dentists, psychologists, social workers, and counselors. It investigates allegations of illegal or unethical conduct by licensees and may sanction licensees including the suspension, restriction, or revocation of licenses.

C **certification:** A determination by a utilization review organization or a health plan that an admission, extension of stay, or other healthcare service has been reviewed and, based on the information provided, meets the clinical requirements for *medical necessity, appropriateness of care,* *level of care,* or *effectiveness,* according to the guidelines of the applicable health benefit plan.

claims denial: An adverse decision regarding the payment to a member for services determined to be not *medically necessary,* services received without prior *authorization, out-of-area/out-of-network* services, or other reasons that violate the payment protocols.

complaint: An oral or written expression of dissatisfaction by an MCO member regarding a specified problem or issue. A complaint does not involve a request for a formal *grievance* or appeals hearing. MCOs must track and document complaints and their resolutions, utilizing this information in quality assurance processes. This information is also reported to regulatory bodies and is increasingly used in so-called *report cards* used by consumers in selecting MCO benefit plans and healthcare delivery systems.

contract credentialing organization: An organization that provides credentialing services under an administrative services contract to a health plan or MCO. Early generations of MCOs often performed this function in-house. As the MCO industry has grown, specialty companies have arisen to manage these processes as subcontractors to MCOs.

credentialing: Process of checking multiple aspects of a physician's (or any other professional provider's) education, background, credentials, and litigation history to ensure quality, competent, and safe care for patients. Eligibility is determined by the extent to which providers meet defined requirements for education, licensure, professional standing, service availability and accessibility, and conformance with managed care organization utilization and quality management requirements.

criteria: Predetermined elements related to particular healthcare services by which the aspects of the *quality,* the *medical neces-*

sity, and the *appropriateness* of a healthcare service may be assessed by healthcare professionals other than physicians. Healthcare professionals relying on professional expertise, prior experience, treatment outcomes information, and the professional literature have developed these criteria. (For example, criteria for admission may involve specific ICD-9 or DSM-IV diagnoses.)

D **days (or visits) per 1,000:** An indicator calculated by taking the total number of days (for inpatient, residential, or partial hospitalization) or visits (for outpatient services) received by a specific group for a specific period of time. To obtain this rate, one must first determine the number of days or visits over a given period; for example, one month. Then divide by the average number of covered members or lives in that group during the same period and multiply by 12,000. This is a key measurement used to evaluate utilization management performance and the overall utilization of services by a given population. For example: ACME MCO experienced 100 bed days for its 30,000 members last month; 100 divided by 30,000 times 12,000 equals 40 days per 1,000 members on an annual basis.

delegation: A formal process by which a managed care organization gives another entity the authority to perform certain functions on its behalf, such as credentialing, utilization management, and quality improvement. Although a managed healthcare organization can delegate the authority to perform a function, it cannot delegate the responsibility for ensuring that the function is performed appropriately.

denial: An initial adverse payment determination by the MCO's care managers based upon documentation demonstrating the lack of *medical necessity,* reasonableness, or *appropriateness,* of healthcare services provided or proposed to be provided to a covered member. Policies and protocols concerning denials, including the member's right to contest the denial must be documented and available to the member.

diagnostic-related group (DRG): One of the 477 clinically meaningful groups into which hospital admissions are classified. The groups are based on a patient's diagnosis, procedures, age, sex, and discharge status under a statistical classification scheme that groups diagnostic categories related to body organ systems and surgical procedures. The classification scheme utilizes categories of diagnoses that should require very similar programs of treatment and lengths of hospital stays. DRGs are used to determine the amount that Medicare reimburses for hospital stays. DRGs were developed at Yale University in 1975 and have been adopted by several states.

disciplinary action: The overall process that includes a proceeding to address network problems and issues with individual participating practitioners, allowing due process for the practitioners. A disciplinary action can possibly result in *sanctions* being imposed on the practitioners by the network.

Division of Health Standards and Quality: A department of the Health Care Financing Administration (HCFA) under the auspices of the Department of Health and Human Services (DHHS).

DRG creep: Practice of coding more resource intensive conditions than are justified by the medical record in order to receive reimbursement in a higher-paying DRG.

DRG validation: A form of review in which the diagnostic and procedural information that is reported by the hospital that results in a DRG assignment is validated by determining whether the information matches the diagnostic and procedural information and data in the member's medical records. DRG validation also includes determining whether the attending physician has attended to the *principal* and *secondary diagnoses*, and whether the procedures ordered and/or performed are appropriate for the diagnoses.

drug utilization review (DUR): Either concurrent or retrospective management of an insured group's medication usage. The goal of such management is to reduce the cost of drug therapies. Methods used to manage drug utilization include: substituting *generic drugs* for name brands, using a formulary to limit the universe of drugs that can be prescribed, using *copayments* for prescriptions, and encouraging the use of drugs that will result in rebates or discounts. (See also *reviews.*)

G **grievance/grievance procedure:** A formal written request by a member for a hearing by the health plan with the aim of reviewing a denial for coverage or other decision adverse to the member. The grievance may regard a *complaint* about care or services received from the plan or a plan provider, or it may involve an *appeal* of a decision made by the plan with regard to the provision of a requested service. Such processes and procedures are generally mandated by state or federal law or by accreditation bodies.

gross and flagrant violation: A violation that occurs when hospitals or healthcare practitioners fail to comply with obligations to a patient, resulting in an imminent danger to the patient.

H **health employer data information set (HEDIS):** A set of standard performance measures developed for managed care plans by the *National Committee on Quality Assurance* (NCQA). It is essentially a report card for managed care plans that allows the consumer to understand what value their healthcare dollar is purchasing and how to hold a health plan accountable for its performance. The standard measures include quality of care, membership and utilization, management and activities, finance, and member access and satisfaction. HEDIS is a registered trademark of NCQA.

health services denial: Adverse decision for the approval of services requested by a member because service was not *medically necessary*, not the *appropriate* treatment for the diagnosis, not a covered benefit, or requested by an *out-of-area* or *out-of-network* provider.

Health Standards Quality Bureau: The branch of *HCFA* with direct oversight for the *peer review organization* program.

I **indicator:** A defined, measurable variable used to monitor the *quality* or *appropriateness* of an important aspect of patient care or service. Indicators can be activities, events, occurrences, or outcomes for which data can be collected to allow comparison with a threshold, a *benchmark*, or prior performance. Clinical indicators are of two types: *outcome* indicators and *process* indicators. Outcome indicators are incidence or prevalence rates for desirable or undesirable health status outcomes, such as infant mortality. Process indicators are usually measures of clinical performance, based on objective clinical criteria defined from *practice guidelines* or other clinical specifications, such as immunization rates.

insurance denial: An adverse payment determination that is issued to a contracted or noncontracted facility, denying payment to a facility due to inappropriate admission, inappropriate care, lack of medical necessity for a continued stay in an acute setting, or for delay of service.

intensified review: An increase in PRO review activity in a specific or general area when a provider and/or practitioner demonstrates a pattern of inappropriate or unnecessary care.

J **Joint Commission on Accreditation of Healthcare Organizations (JCAHO):** Accreditation body that sets standards for hospitals and other health facilities and providers. Standards include staff education, training, patient care, safety procedures, infection control, and others.

L **length of stay:** Time authorized for inpatient hospital days as indicated by the medical condition and diagnosis of the member.

level of care classifications: Refers to the settings for various treatment services along a continuum. MCOs strive to place clients in the least restrictive level of care needed to safely and effectively treat the clients' presenting problem. MCOs utilize clinical care criteria decision trees in making such level of care placement decisions.

M **measure:** A quantifiable element of performance that can be compared to the same element of other performances, such as a dimension of a function, process, or outcome. Measures can be activities, events, occurrences, or outcomes for which data can be collected to allow comparison with a threshold, a *benchmark*, or prior performance.

Clinical measures are of two types. *Outcome* measures are incidence and prevalence rates for desirable or undesirable health status outcomes. *Process* measures are usually of clinical performance, based on objective clinical criteria defined from *practice guidelines* of their clinical specifications.

medical management programs: An inclusive term referring to the plan's utilization management, quality management and credentialing programs, and complaint and grievance resolution. These programs are designed to ensure that members receive appropriate healthcare services.

medically necessary: A treatment or evaluation for a particular condition is determined to be medically necessary by the health plan when the treatment or evaluation is required and appropriate and in agreement with acceptable standards of medical practice. Additionally, the treatment or evaluation cannot be provided in a less intensive setting.

National Committee on Quality Assurance (NCQA): Established as an independent, nonprofit accreditation organization, NCQA began the voluntary accreditation of HMOs in 1991. Today it is the nation's most prominent accreditation body for the managed care industry and its accreditation has become the field's quality benchmark. In 1997 NCQA announced accreditation standards for managed behavioral care organizations and other specialized certification programs.

noncoverage notice review: A review of the member's medical records to determine whether a noncoverage notice was issued to the member. Additionally, the review determines if the notice was issued, if it was issued appropriately, if it contained the appropriate information, and if the hospital appropriately notified the *peer review organization* of the issuance.

notice of noncoverage: A written notice issued by a provider to a member that the healthcare services proposed will not be covered by the insurance, as they are not *medically necessary* or *appropriate*. The services, if provided, would be the financial responsibility of the member.

notice of organizational determination: A letter issued by the *peer review organization* that outlines an adverse denial determination. The letter is issued to the member with a copy to the attending physician and hospital.

O **overutilization:** Deals with situations in which a member is given treatment, therapy, medications etc., which are not necessary for his/her diagnosis.

P **peer review organization/professional review organization (PRO):** an entity that evaluates the appropriateness or quality of a service utilizing professionals of comparable training. Often used in connection with entities that contract with HCFA for the review of services funded by Medicare.

performance goals: The desired level of achievement of standards of care or service. These may be expressed as desired minimum performance levels (thresholds), industry best performance (benchmark), or the permitted variance from the standard.

Performance goals usually are not static, but change as performance improves and/or the standard of care is refined.

performance measurements: A specific measure of how well a health plan does in providing healthcare services to its members. Performance measurements may also be established by employers for their managed behavioral care programs or employee assistance programs. Such measurements may relate to patient satisfaction, service standards, claims payment proficiencies, and treatment outcomes.

population-based study: An analysis that measures compliance with a quality indicator across all at-risk members in the organization. For example, a population-based pediatric immunization study includes all at-risk member children in the denominator of the compliance rate, not just those who have accessed a health delivery site.

primary source verification: Occurs when a managed care company confirms the healthcare practitioner's credentials based upon evidence obtained from the issuing source of the credential.

principal reason(s): A clinical or nonclinical statement describing the general reason(s) for the determination of noncertification. Lack of *medical necessity* is not a sufficient reason for noncertification determination.

Q **quality:** The degree of conformity to a standard. In the case of hospitals, standards of both effectiveness and efficiency must be addressed.

quality assessment: Measurement and evaluation of the quality of medical or behavioral care for individuals, groups, or populations.

quality assurance: A formal set of activities to review and safeguard the quality of medical services provided. Quality assurance involves quality assessment and implementation of corrective actions to address any deficiencies identified in the quality of care and services provided to individuals or populations.

quality control: The process of assessing quality performance, comparing that performance control with the standards, and then acting on the difference.

quality improvement: The effort to assess and improve the level of performance of key processes and outcomes within an organization. Opportunities to improve care and service are found primarily by examining the systems and processes by which care and services are provided. A quality improvement program description is a written description of the organization's quality improvement program that has been approved by the governing body and periodically reviewed and revised as necessary. A quality improvement work plan is an annual plan that describes with timelines the specific planned quality improvement activities that will be carried out within the quality improvement program.

quality management program: A structured program that monitors and evaluates the *quality* and effectiveness of a healthcare system's services. Minimal components include the monitoring of *utilization* of services, *accessibility* of services, *patient satisfaction*, provider *credentialing*, and treatment outcomes. The monitoring component may include chart audits and case reviews. Provider contracts with healthcare systems usually stipulate compliance and cooperation with quality management program activities. The quality management process must include evaluation and educational components to identify and correct problems in the delivery of healthcare.

quality of care: The extent to which services provided by the health plan and its providers are consistent with current *standards of care* and contribute to optimum health outcomes.

quality of services: The extent to which services provided by the health plan and its network of providers meet the reasonable expectations of members for timely, efficient, and courteous services.

quality review: Evaluation of a member's medical records to ensure that the care delivered is consistent with objective medical care assessment. This review includes analysis, intervention, follow-up, and problem resolution.

R **reasonable and necessary:** A term applied to healthcare services considered for payment. For a service to be reasonable and necessary, it must be provided at the appropriate *level of care*, limited to diagnostic evaluation and/or treatment methods relating to the member's condition, must qualify as being a generally accepted practice by the healthcare community, and must be generally recognized as safe and effective.

reconsideration: A request for additional review of a utilization review determination not to certify. The peer reviewer, who reviewed the original decision, based on submission of additional information and/or a peer-to-peer discussion performs this review.

review of service request: A review of information submitted to the utilization review organization (URO) for healthcare services that do not need medical necessity certification or result in a noncertification decision.

reviews:

- **concurrent review:** Utilization review conducted during the patient's course of treatment. A concurrent review determines *medical necessity* or *appropriateness* of services as they are being rendered. For example, a concurrent review can be used to assess the need for continued inpatient care for hospitalized patients. Also termed *continued stay review.*

- **initial or first level review:** The initial review of a request for benefit coverage. Usually conducted by a nurse or other licensed professional.

- **prospective review:** Utilization review conducted prior to a patient's admission, hospital stay, physician services, or other service or course of treatment. Also known as *precertification review.*

- **retrospective review:** Review conducted after services have been provided.

- **second level review:** An appeal review of a request for benefit certification that was denied by the initial review which is conducted by a clinical peer.

- **third level review (expedited appeal):** A request for an additional review conducted by a second peer reviewer who was not involved in the original decision.

risk management: A program undertaken by a health plan or an organization to reduce and/or prevent losses resulting from injuries to members. Such a program may include the identification, analysis, and evaluation of areas of potential loss, as well as addressing specific incidents that may result in loss.

S **sanctions:** Penalties imposed by companies on practitioners participating in the provider network who fail to abide by contracted administrative and medical management requirements, criteria, or standards. Such penalties may include fines, requiring the practitioner to participate in a specific program of remedial education, or suspension or termination of the practitioner's *network* participation status.

secondary source verification: Confirmation by the health plan or organization of the credentials of a healthcare provider based upon evidence obtained by means other than direct contact with the issuing power of the credential. For example, accepting copies of licenses and certifications rather than direct confirmation from the credentialing body.

severity of illness/intensity of service criteria (SI/IS): Universally recognized criteria for utilization review assessment.

standards: Authoritative statements of minimum levels of acceptable performance or results, excellent levels of performance or results, or the range of acceptable performance or results.

substantial violation: A failure of providers or staff healthcare practitioners to substantially meet obligations to a beneficiary in a significant number of cases.

T **threshold for evaluation:** The base or minimum acceptable level of performance, often perceived as a starting point.

U **underutilization:** The failure to provide appropriate and/or indicated services, or provision of an inadequate quantity or lower level of services than required.

utilization: A measurement that may be expressed in a variety of ways. The extent to which a given group uses specified services in a specified period, expressed as the number of services used per year per 1,000 or per 1,000 persons eligible for the services. Utilization rates may be expressed in other types of ratios; e.g., per eligible persons covered. It is the extent to which the members of a covered group use specified services over a specific period, in the aggregate; usually expressed as the number of services used per year. Utilization rates are established to help in comprehensive health planning, budget review, and cost containment.

utilization management: The process of evaluation and determination of the appropriateness of the utilization of medical care resources, and the provision of any needed assistance to clinicians and/or patients in cooperation with other parties (including patients, practitioners, employers, payers) to ensure appropriate use of resources. UM includes *prior authorization, concurrent review, retrospective review, discharge planning,* and *care management.*

utilization rate: The number of employees seen by the healthcare provider divided by the number of employees in the group or company covered by the benefits.

utilization review: A formal evaluation (prospective, concurrent, or retrospective) of the *medical necessity, efficiency,* and/or *appropriateness* of healthcare services and treatment plans.

utilization review organization (URO): An entity that conducts utilization reviews.

Appendix

Health Information Resources

The following is a list of resources that provide information on healthcare, managed healthcare, healthcare policy, and insurance.

HEALTHCARE ORGANIZATIONS

American Association of Health Plans
1129 20th Street, NW, Suite 600
Washington, DC 20036-3421
(202) 778-3200
Internet address: http://www.aahp.org

American Health Care Association
1201 L Street, NW
Washington, DC 20005
(202) 842-4444
Internet address: http://www.social.com

American Insurance Association
Suite 1000
1130 Connecticut Avenue, NW
Washington, DC 20036
(202) 828-7100
Internet address: http://www.aiadc.org

American Managed Behavioral Health Association (AMBHA)
700 13th Street, NW, Suite 950
Washington, DC 20005
Fax: (202) 434-4564
Internet address: http://www.ambha.org

American Medical Association
535 N. Dearborn Street
Chicago, IL 60610-0946
(312) 645-5000
Internet address: http://www.ama-assn.org

American Psychological Association
750 1st Street, NE
Washington, DC 20002
(202) 336-5500
Internet address: http://www.apa.org

The Commonwealth Fund
1 East 75th Street
New York, NY 10021-2692
(212) 535-0400
Internet address: http://www.cmwf.org

Health Administration Responsibility Project (HARP)
5552 12th Street
Santa Monica, CA 90402-2908
Internet address: http://www.harp.org

Health Insurance Association of America
1025 Connecticut Avenue
Washington, DC 20004-2599
(202) 223-2599
Internet address: http://www.hiaa.org

National Association of Social Workers (NASW)
750 First Street, NE, Suite 700
Washington, DC 20002-4241
(202) 408-8600
Fax: (202) 336-8311
Internet address: http://www.naswdc.org

INTERNET RESOURCES

Achoo: Healthcare information resource for the medical
community and all other Internet users.
Internet address: http://www.achoo.com

Healthfinder: A consumer health and human services
information Web site from the United States government.
Internet address: http://www.healthfinder.gov

Institute for Behavioral Healthcare: A nonprofit educational
organization that sponsors continuing education for mental
health, chemical dependency, and substance abuse treatment
providers in the United States and Canada.
Internet address: http://www.ibh.com

Internet Mental Health: A free encyclopedia of mental health
information.
Internet address: http://www.mentalhealth.com

Medscape: Free full text articles for health professionals and
interested consumers.
Internet address: http://www.medscape.com

Mental Health Net: A comprehensive guide to mental health
online—featuring 6,000 individual resources.
Internet address: http://www.cmhsys.com

MANAGED CARE ORGANIZATIONS

ACCESS Care Inc.
Acorn Behavioral Health
ACORN Building
134 N. Narberth Avenue
Narberth, PA 19072
(800) 223-7050
Internet address: http://www.mhsource.com

AETNA/US Healthcare
Aetna Inc.
151 Farmington Ave.
Hartford, CT 06156
(860) 273-0123
Internet address: http://www.aetnaushc.com

Blue Cross/Blue Shield
676 N. Saint Clair Street
Chicago, IL 60611
(312) 440-6000
Internet address: http://www.bluecares.com

CIGNA HealthCare
950 Cottage Grove Road
Bloomfield, CT 06002-2908
(860) 769-4500
Internet address: http://www.cigna.com

ComPsych Behavioral Health Corporation
515 North State Street, #2310
Chicago, IL 60610
(312) 245-2699
Internet address: http://www.compsych.com

Humana
500 W. Main Street
Louisville, KY 40202
(502) 580-1000
Internet address: http://www.humana.com

Kaiser Permanente
Ordway Building
One Kaiser Plaza
Oakland, CA 94612
Internet address: http://www.kaiperm.org

Pacificare Health Systems, Inc.
3120 Lake Center Drive
Santa Ana, CA 92704
(714) 825-5233
Internet address: http://www.phs.com

Prudential HealthCare
56 Livingston Ave.
Roseland, NJ 07068
(973) 716-8000
Internet address: http://www.prudential.com

United Healthcare Corp.
P.O. Box 1459
Minneapolis, MN 55440-1459
(612) 797-4787
Internet address: http://www.uhc.com

Vista Behavioral Health Plans
P.O. Box 1570
Merrifield, VA 22116
(703) 528-2255
Internet address: http://www.vistabhp.org

GOVERNMENT AGENCIES

Agency for Health Care Policy and Research (AHCPR)
Executive Office Center, Suite 600
2101 E. Jefferson Street
Rockville, MD 20852
Internet address: http://www.ahcpr.gov

Bureau of Labor Statistics
441 G. Street, NW
Washington, DC 20210
(202) 523-1222
Internet address: http://www.stats.bls.gov

Centers for Disease Control
1600 Clifton Road, NE
Atlanta, GA 30333
(404) 639-3311
Internet address: http://www.cdc.gov

Department of Commerce
Main Commerce Building
14th and Constitution Avenue, NW
Washington, DC 20230
(202) 377-2000
Internet address: http://www.doc.gov

Department of Health and Human Services
200 Independence Avenue
Washington, DC 20201
(202) 619-0287
Internet address: http://www.os.dhhs.gov

Department of Labor
200 Constitution Avenue NW
Washington, DC 20210
(202) 523-6666
Internet address: http://www.dol.gov

Health Care Financing Administration
6324 Security Boulevard
Baltimore, MD 21207
(310) 966-3000
Internet address: http://www.hcfa.gov

National Center of Health Statistics
3700 East-West Highway
Hyattsville, MD 20782
(301) 436-8500
Internet address: http://www.cdc.gov/nchwww/nchshome

National Health Information Center
P.O. Box 1133
Washington, DC 20013-1133
(800) 336-4979 or (301) 565-4167
Internet address: http://www.nhicnt.health.org

National Institutes of Health
9000 Rockville Pike
Bethesda, MD 20892
(301) 496-4000
Internet address: http://www.nih.gov

Pension and Welfare Benefits Administration
200 Constitution Avenue, NW
Washington, DC 20216
(202) 523-8921
Internet address: http://www.dol.gov/pwba

Social Security Administration
6401 Security Boulevard
Baltimore, MD 21235
(301) 594-6660
Internet address: http://www.ssa.gov

Substance Abuse and Mental Health Services Administration
   (SAMHSA)
Parklawn Building
5600 Fishers Lane
Rockville, MD 20857
(301) 443-3783
Internet address: http://www.samhsa.gov

Directory of MCO
Quality Oversight Organizations

**Council on Accreditation of Services for Families
and Children, Inc. (COA)**
520 Eighth Avenue, Suite 2202B
New York, NY 10018
Phone: (212) 797-3000
Fax: (212) 797-1428
Internet address: N/A

The largest independent accrediting body for agencies, providing social and mental health services to families, children, and other individuals. COA also accredits agencies with a formal EAP component.

**The Council on Quality and Leadership in Supports
for People with Disabilities (The Council)**
100 West Road, Suite 406
Towson, MD 21204
Phone: 410/583-0060
Fax: 410/583-0063
Internet address: http://www.accredcouncil.org

The Council is a diversified quality enhancement organization with an international focus in the field of human services, dedicated to ensuring that people with disabilities have full and abundant lives.

**Joint Commission on Accreditation of Healthcare
Organizations (JCAHO)**
1 Renaissance Boulevard
Oakbrook Terrace, IL 60181

Phone: (708) 916-5790
Fax: (708) 916-5644
Internet address: http://www.jcaho.org

The Joint Commission is the primary standard-setting organization in both inpatient and outpatient mental health treatment centers and other healthcare organizations.

National Committee for Quality Assurance (NCQA)

2000 L. Street, NW, Suite 500
Washington, DC 20036
Phone: (202) 955-3500
Fax: (202) 955-3359
Internet address: http://www.ncqa.org

NCQA accredits managed behavioral healthcare organizations.

Utilization Review Accreditation Commission (URAC)

1275 K Street, Suite 100
Washington, DC 20005
Phone: (202) 216-9010
Fax: (202) 216-9006
Internet address: http://www.urac.org

A nonprofit corporation established to encourage more efficient and effective utilization review and utilization management process by providing for private accreditation of utilization management forms through the use of national utilization review standards.